AF480144

Water Rock Time

Also by Don Langford

In the Light of the Full Moon: Dispersions, Glimpses, and Reflections

Songs from Deep Time

Dwelling in the Twilight Realm

Water Rock Time

Poems by

Don Langford

Published by D S Langford Publishing
Columbus, OH 43229
https://dslangfordpublishing.com

Printed in the United States

Cover Design by Don Langford, 2024

Names: Langford, Don, author
Title: *Water Rock Time* / Don Langford

ISBN 979-8-9867546-7-3 (pbk)
ISBN 979-8-9867546-8-0 (eBook)

Library of Congress Control Number: 2024907944

First Printing, May 2024

For Marlene, always inspiring creativity

The night is fresh and cool—
Staff in hand, I walk through the gate,
Wisteria and ivy grow together along the winding
    mountain path;
Birds sing quietly in their nests and a monkey
    howls nearby.
As I reach a high peak a village appears in the distance.
The old pines are full of poems;
I bend down for a drink of pure spring water.
There is a gentle breeze, and the round moon hangs overhead.
Standing by a deserted building,
I pretend to be a crane softly floating among the clouds.

Ryokan (1758-1831)

While everyone else
is so busy striving,
the lone traveler
is at ese by himself.
He's been living outside of convention
for a long time now;
in his pouch there is nothing at all.
When he walks,
he takes a cane for a companion;
when he talks,
he has the rocks for an audience.
If you ask him what his religion is,
when hungry it's a bowl of rice.

Wen-siang (1210-1288)
(Translated by Thomas Cleary)

Contents

Part 3: Time

Part 1: Water

Desert Sky

Today, gentle rain
        tapping
        like children's fingers on the roof.

At sunset, the underside
        of folded clouds
        golden, rolling east
              over mountains
              and valley.

Hot Mineral Bath

Cool morning
         in California desert
         sitting in hot mineral bath
         cradled in its warm liquid embrace

These steaming pools have deep thermal ties
         to ancient seas and molten ores

Water, flesh and bone
         sharing common origins,
         flowing together for a time

The Tanager's Song

The summer tanager's soft
and clear song
calls to me
to turn my eyes outward
and see what is here

Today it is morning fog
and lively tunes
of food gathering
and nest building
after the night's rainy storm

In the near distance
a wooded bog
of singing frogs,
last night's chorus
soft as wave-like winds

From the gray muted softness of light
shadow-like tree trunks emerge,
green-gray needles disappearing high above
in the deeper gray of sky

The birds and squirrels here
live among the forests and campers,
seeing and hearing their own worlds
as we see ours

At times in the overlapping
a bird cocks its head
looking with one eye, then the other
at a person standing still
or passing by

But here they remain wild
and do not approach, seeking food,
as the seagulls do
along the coastal shore

Here the chirping
that crosses our ears
is meant for other birds
and we just listen quietly
to their pleasing song

After the Rain

After the rain
children ride bicycles
through ruts and mud puddles
laughing and splashing,
barking at the dogs
to get them going

In the afternoon,
mud-caked boots
piled in a heap,
dirty bikes waiting
for another ride

Returning to the Source

Standing at the headwaters of the Metolius,
water bubbling up,
leaking out of the ground
more of a trickle than a flow

Humble origins,
late bloomer from the north
like snow-ball rolling

gradual and persistent
growing on its downhill ride,
      someday arriving
         at the sea

A Little Frozen Pond

We were children once,
and in the faintness of memory
there was a shallow pond
far back behind the house

We played in the bush
and in tall fragrant grasses
with our little dog

And there were wild pear trees
around the old concrete foundation
of a burned-out house
that we never tired of visiting;
a crumbling fireplace and chimney
reminded us that someone once lived there

When the small pond froze over
in the winter we put on our ice skates
and our caps and mittens
and stepped from the frozen golden grasses
on to the thick and crackling slab of ice
to play all afternoon
until our hands were numb
and the cuffs of our pants
were ice-caked in stiff frozen folds

Tell me, do children today
still toboggan down those old frozen roadways
or run aimlessly far from home
with their dogs through long carefree afternoons,
and in the summer
do they wait with dimes and quarters
clenched tightly in their hands
for the ice cream truck to arrive,

or hear the beverage truck bringing wooden crates
of mixed flavored pop, bottles jangling
all the way down the street,
straight to the house?

What are the safe and comforting memories
today's children will someday recall
of their own long-ago summers and winters?

Beyond the Shoreline View

Beneath the ocean's surface
the strong currents swirl;
even the signs warn us
be aware of rip currents

And those posted signs
advise us not to struggle
against the forces beneath the surface;
allow them to guide you, they say,
to the safest zones;
do not exhaust yourself
in fighting against the deep currents

The undercurrents of the ocean
are vast and ancient
like the oldest mind
beneath surface awareness

Sitting on the sandy shore
looking out to sea
we rarely see its force;
it is when we enter
past the shoreline waves
that we feel its push and pull

In our direct contact
we learn something of its force
like deep intellect
operating beneath the mental surface
of our shoreline view

The Wateryness of Meaning

The watery-ness of words,
        fluid rivers of meaning,
        pooling concepts
        coursing recklessly toward obstruction,
        damming the range of flow

We try again, reiterating in iterative approximations,
        defending our claim:
        all utterances are not the sensations
        they attempt to translate;
        they do not equate or equivocate

Lost in the eddies that swirl
        around ideas and emotions;
        lost in the riptides that pull us
                away from what is most important,
                the fundamentals of our
                        being here

The little rivulets we tried to follow
        long before any wordiness of vision
                intervened, even interrupted,
                occasionally contravened,
                and even contested

Now the language interferes
        with where we want to go
        in this inquiry into the meaningful,
                before the fragmentarians among us
                tried to pull us apart

A disquisition of this sort, *in situ*, should dive deeply
        into the aqueous world of words, splitting molecules, if necessary,
        so hydrogen is liberated from its filial bond,
        hurtling closer toward pure meaning

We incubate a surrogate brood of words and images
        that have severed (cleaved if you like) the umbilical
        toward a more restrictive language that would have
                oxygen become the dominant bond-mate as water tumbles
                like bubbling plosives over riverbed stones to the sea

What we wanted, after all, was to have some wordless affirmation
        of our discourses, some semblance of watery resolution
                of our most consequential certainties
                in this ever-flow of wordiness

Ocean to Ocean

Our travels now take us inland
away from the eastern ocean and great waves;
away from the great gulf coast
and its fine white sandy beaches

Already we see the young reddening buds
and earliest blooms of spring
filling out trees in the Deep South

The year will be late and the leaves golden
when we reach the northwestern waters
where the dew-damp mists
quench the dense evergreen conifers

We pass through lands labeled
        with stories of human history
        even as we live in our own time
                which, too, lives in history

How much older these seas and forests
        whose histories we look upon,
        marvelling when we sit, absorbed
        at every sunset, with some deep wonder
        that has its own long human history

Cool Water

Narrow woodland creek.

      Winding silky water flow

           over smooth gray rounded stones.

Cool downward swirl.

      Bubbles. Gurgling ripples.

Irresistible.
Cupped hands dipping
      to touch
      to feel

      to lift cool water
         to face
      in the filtered morning light.

Behind the River

I no longer remember the names of muscles
and still I stretch
each morning and afternoon
from long habit and routine

Many years ago the nearby river
changed its course
from timber fall and sliding rock
and still it flows

The name we give
to the invisible unwavering principle
is "the Way"
but that is just a name
like "nature's law,"
the way "trapezius"
is not the forgotten muscle
or "Vesuvius" the old volcanic form

And when I sit long hours
beside the river
the "I" and "river" and "long hours"
are only names that fall away
like mid-morning fog
evaporating in the air

What remains always
behind the forms and names
and the many other uttered words
is the nameless ungraspable Way,
arising alongside this wonder-filled world
        of appearances

At Steinhagen Lake

A finger-thin rock-studded jetty
juts into Steinhagen Lake
where we stand above shiny wind-blown wavelets
gazing upon the swampy banks,
and farther out beyond
this compass needle-point of land,
past the bone-white trees stippled in the watery glaze
toward a distant horizon

We are visitors to this place,
guests we might say,
to all the places
we inhabit for a short time

In our house on wheels
we travel alone,
without caravan,
using the tools of our time
to navigate our way
in a freedom we have chosen

In our travels from place to place,
we awaken some mornings
to views outside our windows
that are a surprise to us,
as if we had expected
the scene from days before

Beneath the pin oaks and maples,
our view in the morning
rests upon a golden-brown carpet
of last autumn's curled and fallen leaves
draped over an undulating lawn
here at the edge of winter and spring,

as tiny red buds
dot the branches above,
signals of the newest unfurling sprouts,
life's verdant harbingers of a new and welcomed season

Refreshing Winter Snow

There were times
along the winter hiking trails,
long before the forever chemicals
invaded the skies and earth,
that we scooped the crusty snow
into our tin cups and thermoses,
and further along the way
sloshing around inside our packs
it melted over a sprig of mint
as we trudged along the trail;

later when we stopped to rest,
leaning against a stone or sitting on a fallen tree,
we enjoyed the cool refreshing taste,
smelled the breezy fragrant pine
and listened to the softness of air
passing through a million green needles
singing to us from mountain and sky.

In a Pool after the Rain

Even in the crowded campgrounds
we had the swimming pool to ourselves
immediately after a rain
when the air was still cool
and puddles had not yet dried

Sometimes a few drops of rain
continued to fall
while we floated on our backs
in the cool and silky water

We imagined holding open our umbrellas,
to shield us from the softly falling drops
and giggling as we paddled on our backs
graceful in the healing waters
floating from one end to the other

One Fine Morning

We drove past tired mansions
with their colors of dust

spidery suburbs, radiant
in their long slow decay

past the wonderlands
lusting toward senility
in never-ending desire
in the morning sunlight

a cityscape of tall leaning shadows
twisted into grotesque metallic grays
spread against the long lonely sky

We are leaving again
this our home
at last
always leaving
          again, alone

never hesitant
in our impulse

this is where we always return
these modern tenements
ant colonies of love
and jazz
playing the tune
          of always
and possibilities
to the tune of
          keep me here
and the wailings of we need you

ever desirous
even in the tirades
the sweeping gestures of the heart
the melodious facsimiles of love
always returning

even before that old sinking sun
reaches the sandy shore
where the striped umbrellas
lean one more time
dreaming of the sea

Calibrio *in Absentia*

In the one note
water's vibrational waves,
fields without boundaries

One arm lets go
        the other holds on

Lifting mists reveal mountains
        first of doubt
        then wonder

Not having seen the sea
        we bring only sand
        and eyes of what might have been

A break in the clouds
        carved stone faces
        rest in the wind

From water-woven reeds
        shapes appear to carry water
                then fire in the stones

Exuded from one note
        enfolded in silence
        bright wakeful morning

Sonorous Rhythms

Skipping stones across water
      one two three
      rings and circles on the surface

Pulsations emanating, receding
      lakes and oceans related
      like aunts and uncles
      in lapping tidal inflow rhythm

Ancient heroes had no names
      for day of week
      or time of day

Seeing the same stones
      skipping in sonorous rhythms
      without distractions accumulating

Standing at the water's edge
      a moment shared
      across the sky's vast expanse

Ontogeny of the Tendril

Beautiful green leaves
of palm and ficus

tall and broad
beyond the measure
        of climbing

pulling water upward
        into gravity's outer canopy

deep-rooted fibrous filaments
        collecting each its smallest portion
        gaining complexity with size

        like the ant colony
        building intricate tunnels
        beyond a single ant's ability

and we too send tendrils outward
        to moon and mars

        the capillaries
        of our human colony
        pushing star-ward
        beyond the bounds
        of our knowing

When the Travelers Settle Down

We have seen beautiful white-sand Gulf Coast beaches
where tall palm trees share the land
          with pines and short palm ferns;

We saw the breaking waves
          against the hardness of coastal rock face
          along the northern Pacific Coast;

          the deepest blue inland lakes,
          pristine and quiet
          in this time of rapid change;

          the rushing rivers
          still carving their course
          in rapid full flow;

          the muddy Mississippi
          slowly moving soil and barges to sea
          through historic Southern cities

And we have glimpsed only the edges
          of the ocean's vastness

There are thousands of islands and coves
          yet unseen, like fruits yet untasted

So much paradise remains unseen,
          unfathomed experiences,
          places beyond our imaginings,
          the unaccomplished destinations

And what of the unseen?
So many travelers tell us
they grow content to settle again in place

or travel in smaller orbits,
slowing the pace,
appreciative of what they have seen
enriched, too,
and nothing to prove to themselves
or to others

The calm contentedness in their voices,
relaxing into the weary bones,
now soaking in still waters
or healing with a slower gait

Their memories wait for occasions
to be unlocked, shared with others
in the quiet stillness of reflection

In the Softness of Water

In the softness of water
        we swam

bathing in
        new and deep stillness

finding welcome currents
        rhythms of flowing

smoothing the rough edges
        and sharp turns

        like tumbling hidden gems
        using water's soft burnish

We cascaded through seasons
        looking from quiet eddies
        long enough to see
                leaves emerge
        in green bursts of spring
        outside the windshield
        of our house on wheels

Rolling lawns brightened
        in a dozen shades of green
        children exuberant
        people talking in the distance
        warm friendliness, words indistinguishable,
        blending with birdsong
        from the budding trees

Not cacophony, but soft sound-flow
        pleasant, blending, mellifluous

We swam in place
        in new intent
        taking time
        to slow time

How many seasons have raced by
        without our noticing

Each spring the call and response
        of bird to bird
        leaf to bird
        and fragrance to insects abounding

And we too are welcomed
        by all that we hear and smell
        in the sweet and fragrant air,
        the morning calling us
        in our willful aim to listen,
        to be pliant for a time

Longing at Water's Edge

Why we return to the sea,
the mossy brook,
the lapping wavelets
at the lake's sandy shoreline

endless change
over the monotone surface
the glassy plain
that breeds the wild storms

the sameness pulls us in,
mesmerizing sound loops
cascade over river stones,
or ocean waves on sandy berms,
in slow watery heartbeat rhythms

old stuff, unremembered—
womb music, oneness undivided
longing without return—
we were jettisoned forever out of the waves

we wait on the shoreline
or swim in comforting shallows,
refreshed in this quiet detachment
disguised as home

Part 2: Rock

Mountain Breath Climb

Climbing mountain
     upward is hardness
     toward comfort

tight muscles, burning
     to get
further, stepping sounds
on gravel pebbles
     loose and solid
arms pulling upward
     rock and root

to stop, view
     to see
     breathe clean air
relax, exhaustion
     tightness and blue sky
     drink slow sip
        water
     bow inside, respect

     energy, new refreshed,
     go down slope, care
        and full

To Flatiron on Superstition Mountain

Trudging slowly up Siphon Draw
climbing over boulders, grabbing branches
firmly rooted in rock
         finding a toe-hold
         in the tumble packed tightly
                  in the shaded canyon walls

Pulling, pushing, straining upward
         in aching exhaustion
         toward the goal of Flatiron
         standing high above
         against the blue sky

Resting, back against stone
         breathing hard
         high above valley
         and far-distant mountain ridges,
         for a moment before moving again upward

No need to reach the summit;
this could be enough,
but something pulls upward
         into the unknown

The rock hardens at mid-elevation
then higher up it crumbles
climbing upward through earth time here,
         layers of hot compressed core material
         steps of sharp squared blocks
         burning muscles
         hours of upward climbing

Other hikers point the way
        offer encouragement and water
        before the final hard push to the top

From atop Flatiron
        a distant view, enchanted exhaustion
                its own reward

Joyful satisfaction
        intense, momentary
        inscribed and etched deeply enough
                to go with me all the way
                        back down.

Mountain Sand Granules

The granulated white sand
      on the beach
      we were told
         is granite

Wind and water, persistent,
      eroding solid mountain rock face
      to this fine white sand

On house-sized boulders
      young pine trees grow,
      soft and pliant roots
         burrowing deeply,
         cracking stone

On this wind-blown beach
      we are sprinkling old mountains
      from one hand to another

Tomorrow we climb up the gorge
      to mountain summit;
      granite boulders on the way
      to their destiny:
      beach sand piled high,
         sand dunes for sea oats

The Quiet Traveler

Future gold prospector, rock hound,
        modern-day stone-tumbler,

            dreaming forth a time
            tumbling down roads,
            heading for the tailings

            living his dreams
            one at a time
                    with a
                    heart of gold

In the hot tub, he talks the past,
        sail boating to the Caribbean
        learning new tools,
        knowing so little

            traveling the country
            round winding bends
            seeing canyons, oceans
            skirting the continent,
            living in the open
                    under stars

He is a modest story-teller,
        quiet traveler, soaking in
                this afternoon
        before returning
        to wife and dinner,
        making more dreams real

Earth Resonance

Picture the old man,
wizened and wobbling,
cane outstretched
tapping on stones,
winding his way
upward, old mountain goat,
finding the tunes
radiating deep inside
quartz obelisks

listening patiently
to hear earth music
come to him
from the hollow spaces
with each tap of the stones
along the mountain's meridians

ear to the sounds
hearing sand cymbals
gongs of glass
soft arpeggios
emanating from
invisible lines
through rocks, riverbeds
and whorls of driftwood snags

waves of color
dancing in slow pulsations before the eyes,
rhythmic tonal sprays of sound
subtle as morning mist
evaporating in summer's red heat,
symphony in a single note
all the sounds in a rainbow
slow radiant echoes

dissolving against the canyon walls
as the old man
climbs through the mist line

Our Precipitous Rock Ledge

Resting in morning sun,
lizard-like in our stillness
most basic of animal postures
seated, elemental,
       on a rock
       overlooking
       deep green valley
       where trees stand quietly
       beneath an unforgiving sun

A lesson in patience, it may seem,
       from ridge to ridge
       out to some far distant horizon
       that invites our vision
       to look more closely

Some of the trees have been speaking out;
       this language we understand:
       blighted and dried out forests,
       bark-beetle dead for miles.

Others dry out, parched
       beyond endurance,
       a slow quiet dying
       far from our perch
       on the rock ledge,
       where we watch
       from this precipitous home

The pines are telegraphing to one another
       from root to root their signals
       of stress and disease

Others may yet go up in flames,
     sending toxic plumes
     as their final dying message

And we sit upon our silent rocky ledge,
     not yet ready to hear
     the urgent songs
     sounding all around us;
     not yet seeing the fibrous tree root filaments
     connected to the webbed branches
     of our own lungs

Soft Rock Island

Hard as a lonely island
shaped by an unswerving past
          we wander on

          no going back
          no new way forward
          no undoing the deeds and the demons

The solitary voices
keep tagging along
reminders of road blocks,
          unfulfilled dreams.

Again tonight
a search party wanders
vigilant and untiring
looking for clues,
questioning witnesses
all the way home.

In the waiting and spinning
          orbits and tales
          we fashion new stories,
          catch glimpses of moonlight,
          carve some new masks
          to wear for the travelers
          who ride slowly past us
                    in the comic parade
                    we all star in.

Self-Spinning Conjurer

Eye saw rock
ear heard wind
hand felt hardness and cold,
         sharp corners and edges,
nose smelled dampness;

and mind conjured many ideas
including doubts about
what the wind and hardness
said about the rock,

and how the mental presence
appeared when eye saw rock
and ear heard wind
and hand felt hardness;

that mind said was mine:
my hand, my eye, my ear,
like a conjurer deep inside a tent,
hidden by carpeted partitions,
spinning together the fabric of self

using the eye and ear and hand
as threads woven into a magician's knot,
concealing the conjurer's trick
of spinning self from mind
in its grand deception

Free Form Walking Rock

absorbing the night sky to dreams,
and fleeting, the way the temperament
follows without holding
dedication to the heart and an orange horizon
converting rock-like persistence
into the rim of sunset

letting go and fleeting, the way
dedication to the task
follows its course
oblong in its haste,
mercurial in its demeanor,
converting the night sky to dreams

pushing the sunset in an act of clinging,
the effortless and rounded dome of sky
tempered by orange persistence
follows its dedication, pushing
colonies of absorbed moments
toward tomorrow's daybreak

in the rock fruit and bush land,
determination persists,
echoing the starry feathers
adorning the basilica
dedicated to the lost faces
and all the smiles that grow cold
in the waiting feet that walk
the rainy streets of Rome

Ondine and the Rock Outlasting

Ondine, aglow at nightfall,
dressed in deep subterranean blue,
eyes of ice painted with coal dust
and golden vapor, resting her heels,
nymph-like out of water, leaning
against the city rock at Town Creek
before the street widens

Even the wide-eyed children grin
past the rock, hiding giddy youthful stares,
not yet circumspect nor sheltered
by the lonely hearts yet undiscovered
that await their fading innocence and dreams

Hand stains and polished sheen
of kisses and fingers gloss the rock
that marks the center of town,
a history of sideways glances,
stealthy leanings, before the porticoes
of city hall were fashioned
and burned to the ground;
rock outlasting the comet's passing
and newspaper accounts
of the wealthy and the restless;
the music and fashion,
styles like the trees and their leaves,
bursting in color, fading into softness;
the rock waits in silence,
song birds wait their turn

Pulverized Brick Dust

The morning teases
with its silhouettes
and curving folds
of curtains
in the straining light

They are pointing
to some outward place
where we wanted peace
even as the growing tumult
presaged war

So many bricks
taken from the growing rubble
like the boys sent far away,
disappearing around some corner
while new buildings rise
in the empty footprints

Ideas pulverized into red
brick dust, rock into powder,
fashioned into merchandise
with no burial ground large enough
to cover the memories
that rise like ghosts
from the steaming ground

In the lacy curtain's fold
turning slowly at the open window
a stirring breeze
meets hypnotic stare,
softens a broken heart
that waits for one who does not return

Rock Is Gas in Slow Motion

Rock is gas
      in slow motion

So slow, break a finger
      scratching its hardness

Whirling stone, speed it up
into solid swirling fan blade—
      it severs the finger every time
      even with more space than blade

Speed it up all the way,
      poke a finger
      into a massive gas cloud
      containing inter-mingled bits of space debris

floating far away in distant cold recesses
      where space and black holes
      wait to warm the matter
      in a wide moving swirl
      or disappear down a worm hole
      into unimagined worlds
      of gasified transformation

Swirl it around
      do it again
         see what you get

Cracks in the Rock of Truth

When we traveled
from sun and wind
in nature's slow and even flow
into cities once again for our provisions,
this is what we saw:

Cracks in the rock of truth,
toxic words sowing doubt,
certainties turned poisonous

Even the sleepwalkers
evangelized throughout the night
witnesses provoking the death of dreams

People spoke with certainty
of their fabricated speculations
unmoored from what was once observable

Behind the smiling hospitality
fangs of hidden hatred waited, and
language lay coiled and venomous

We tread carefully in a toxic minefield,
picking up what we needed before departing,
wondering if closely on our heels such hatred followed

This was not the land we came to see,
so full of promise and bloom,
quickly transformed, unrecognizable and fading

While rotting trees seem long in dying,
in time, their fallen hulks feed a future generation
of green and vital shoots and vines
that transform forests into vibrant life again

When Rocks Dissolve

Our foothold slipped,
        first in gravel spray
        then the solid rock face
                slid away
        and we knew we were floating
        with no hard footing
        no safe place for landing

We might have known
our lives were preparations
for this uncovering and rapid release
        of safe retreats

There were premonitions
        when we were young
        that we had either forgotten
        or feared to confront

We pushed back the discomforts
        knowing perhaps that they
                would return
                when the world
        summoned in us some courage
        to look at the horrors we had severed
        in our deep childhood nightmares

We look differently now at solid rocks,
        planted mysteries waiting
        until they too dissolve
        or explode before our welcoming stare

Water Rock Time
(In memory of my mother and father)
2024-03-27

We lived in a time of heroes
          who were rock solid, unwavering,
          always there for us as reminders,
                    as examples
          not dwelling in the clouds
          but here with us, among us

Some were family, others could have been family,
          some—most now—were long ago
          in memory now fading
          returning to mind on occasions like this,
                    remembering

Now we learn our own lessons;
          we do not play the heroes to anyone
          in this solitariness we longed for
          the freedom we desired

          the contentedness we now dwell in

Our friends are the glints in people's eyes
          that we meet in our wanderings
          not in searching, but experiencing

Today we sit with our breath
                    close companion
                    when we remember

Knowing that nothing is rock solid
          or impermeable

There is a softness even in rock
        that the softness of water will penetrate
        given enough time, like patience for those of us
                who are not water, or heroes

Polyvocal Magnum Mysterium por la Cueva

Introito:
Ladies and Gentlemen,
Your Honor,
Boys and Girls, and all our honored guests,
we are gathered here
on this auspicious occasion, truly
a once in a lifetime opportunity
as the time is drawing near.
Some will say the train has left the station,
we can't put the genie back in the bottle, but
it is better late than never, and with a heavy heart
we can count our blessings
dulce et decorum est.
Operators are standing by to take your calls
and there's a line drive to deep left field;
certainly you have every reason to ask
where were you when I needed you
can I go outside and play
is there anybody here to listen to my story
time is short, and the living is easy
there's one thing we can all agree upon
as the storm clouds gather:
it can't happen here, never in a thousand years,
we have every right to make our voices heard
and given enough time and money
I'll get down on my knees,
but first and foremost
let us also remember those who cannot
be with us today, and shout it from the rooftops
before all is said and done,
it is high time that we
get down to brass tacks.

Glissando:
If I've told you once, I've told you a million times,
when you grow up you'll understand these things
this is for your own benefit,
you'll thank me later
I'm telling you for the last time
I'm with you on this
we can accomplish great things
it starts with an idea
the sky's the limit
it's like the wild wild West
water, water everywhere,
and not a holy sphinx

Caesura:
There's no doubt about it:
I think, therefore I am

Crescendo:
Do not make a mockery of our sorrow
painting a rosy crushing picture
of the suffering that has no name
this is going to hurt me more than it hurts you,
we have been dishonored in these chambers
and unfit for human consumption,
and I will not seek re-election.
It is a dastardly act, humiliating beyond recognition,
to be besmirched publicly like this
in these hallowed halls
and dark chambers of the heart
where we have lost our way
in our haste is our beginning
mistakes were made
the last will and testament will be bursting in air
and for every season there is a
rabbit in the hat and a chicken in every pot

Da Capo:
So we have,
through thick and thin skin,
come to the conclusion
that given enough time
the stars are our destiny
and to dust we shall return
a dime a dozen
before this union falls.

Rubato:
There is a train a comin'
and we all need to be on board
with one voice, in *sotto voce*,
where we're preaching to the choir,
in purity of thought
resplendent in purpose and intent,
ardent in illness and in health,
salubrious and gaunt,
where the most formidable will fall
not on a sword, petard, or infamy,
nor on any ill conceptions
or misdemeanors of the heart,
but on the pinnacle of modest achievements
like clawing to a mountain cave
where a mat of papered leaf awaits
alongside a gourd with the purest spring water
and the clearest possible view of valley
that one could ever hope to see.
Make your own nest and lie in it.
Have the courage to be all that you can be.
Make no mistake about it
to tell you the truth,
that is our earnest wish to all of you
on this grotesque and sanguine evening
where so much remains possible.

Many thanks to all of you for coming
in this our darkest hour, on an evening
such as this when you could have
done so much for your country and brethren,
parting the waters on a day that will live in infamy
and last but not beast in the jungle,
to add insult to injuy,
there will be refreshments in the lobby
and bombs bursting in air,
and a book signing where you can procure
your very own autographed copy for a small donation.
Thank you everyone, and Sammy, if you will,
please turn out the lights on your way out.

Part 3: Time

This Wondrous Present Time

There is a kind of waking
that no clock or morning crow
          assists in

Unannounced and unbeckoned it arrives
singular, while we are fully awake
          as if all that has come before
          is suddenly forgotten

It is an intense presence of the Present
often welcomed with joy and wonder

and without words it somehow announces
          or conveys
          here I am
          and here is a world, ready-made

          as if it was the most profound
          discovery or understanding
          that has come our way

It is as if we have been dropped
          into the scene of a play
          or a beauteous landscape
          with some vague obligation
          to figure out how to live
          in this wondrous present time

Time's Reminders

There are reminders
in the sea waves on the sandy shore,
the broken antler found along a meadow's path,
even in the children's high-pitched laughter

All around us, in the slow drip of morning dew,
the rusted truck sinking in a grassy field,
the persistent cough of a loved one,
the exquisite beauty of colorful roadside flowers

We know there are endings of all that we love,
seasons bright with reminders
that we too will fade out of bloom
and perhaps remain for a time in someone's memory
before joining those countless unseen grains
that the sea waves sweep over
in a span far beyond our knowing

Finding a Way

We have chosen to wander
away from the lands of our birth,
then from the homes where we were raised,
and now from the comforts and acquisitions
that bound us for so long

We are not free from entanglements
        and likely never will be,
        just loosening the tethers that bind us still
        to food and the necessaries of life

The idealism of our past had real possibility
        for a time, or so it seemed in some lived way

But today that ideal seems antiquated and sad
        with its assassinations
        and culture of consumption

Only in music and a few outposts
        did the early dreams flourish
        for a time, for a few

The metropolis, once the source of novelty,
        has fallen into decay,
        opportunities now nostalgic;
        and the outposts now import
        the life-draining box stores,
        and the noise and speed that follow

So we travel through landscapes
for which we are no longer the stewards,
seeking the natural and the wild,
where we can touch once again what we always wanted

Back to the Desert

Beneath that old palm tree
in Yuma Arizona
I thought I saw
a maple
from another time

I saw the golden red leaves
undulating in autumn waves
and smelled the musty fresh decay
for a fleeting moment
before the desert heat
          reasserted itself.

Coming to Terms

The path is a crooked line
strewn with feathery barbs
at once inviting as a sunset,
yet bound with ruts
and broken glass that cuts

The path is not earthen soft
nor ox cart quiet,
today it is mad fast and foreign
with concrete, cutoffs, and signage
full of distraction

Ryokan would be driven
to further solitude
or to more soothing saké
by these noisy byways
where few flowers grow

Who adapts to this speed and noise
without losing bearings
or becoming a mad juggler of tasks
racing toward one goal or another
chased by a wailing bell

In this new itinerant life
carrying a home over changing land
turtle-like rabbit
racing from asphalt pad to pad
longing for solitude,
at times traveling
with Fitzcarraldo's overland ship

The idyllic world is in the mind
or posted on seductive highway signs;
this is not the dream
of children playing
and picking flowers

And many home-bound people envy us
in our free and rootless life.
modern gypsy wanderers,
orphaned old travelers
meeting acquaintances
who speak the same language
without sharing the same search

We chose to be itinerants
still tethered to a world
we were running from,
now finding ourselves
bouncing about like bumper cars
in a carnival life we did not intend

Our glimpses of places
remind us of the comings and goings,
the rising and falling away,
the natural disappearances
of all the days and long golden sunsets
while we gain our bearings
in a moving turntable world
without spinning out of orbit

And when we settle into silent places
we accept them with open eyes and arms
knowing that they too will pass
and knowing too that this is not yet the day
when we ease into equanimity
balanced while standing still

like the hummingbird
or waving sea, motion and stillness

We stop long enough
to write the poem
share a word
or walk a desert trail
          or sandy shore
tasting the local fare and air,
then move along
in our sampling
of this spinning world

Stately Old Travelers

In time, the mantle of elder
may be granted

a stately redwood
      or surviving elm
      given a plaque or name

      or scarred by time
      the great majestic humpback whale

or a lone pine
that park rangers
discovered far from any trail

It may be you
whose years crept slowly in youth
then sped through decades
until you found the world had changed

The youth in speed and noise
may not heed your words of wisdom
until they too have seen the years
of accumulation turn to reflection

We return to the wild places
visitors to the only world we know
traveling humble and curious as children
once again with gratitude
to learn from those stately old travelers
who share the road we're on

Celestial Light and Dark
2024-04-01

After a warm Fool's Monday
of yellow pollen dusting the pool where we swam,
tonight we see lightning flashing
in broad bright sheets behind the clouds.

Wind and rain cool the air,
and like curious children
we step wide-eyed into the wind
where light flashes all around us.

We look up and wind ourselves
in slow orbits to see the sky fill
with light and cloudy silhouettes.

This is our sky week as we travel deeper
into the region's hill country
in our modern pilgrimage of wonder
to sit in the new moon's shadow
and feel the rare pull of sun and moon
in mid-day darkness.

With our ancestors' awe
we will watch the shadow race over us
savoring the wonder at seeing such a spectacle.

Buddha-Dharma Practice

The Erlenmeyer flask on the laboratory bench
       held a cloudy liquid
       whether resting or in motion,
       like a distracted mind in constant turmoil,
       unsettled by distraction.

Drip by drip from the pipette
       and long focused stirring and swirling
       wrought no change to the flask's turgid substance.

During continual ceaseless dripping,
       in an instant like a lightning flash,
       one drop, it seemed,
       brought transparent clarity within the flask,
       whether resting or in motion.

A single drop atop the thousands before,
       all necessary to instant transformation.

Dogen writes that "Shakyamuni practiced with difficulty
       and pain for immeasurable aeons
       and finally attained this dharma."

Excellent precedent for practicing buddha-dharma
       "solely for the sake of buddha-dharma."

Waiting for the Tide to Turn

we fed our solitude
            until
the tides receded

we asked ourselves,
who would want
this wondrous gloom,
with its green and scummy sound
racing into the nightfall

forgetting even the reason
for coming to this place
we asked ourselves one more time,

can we escape
before anyone finds us
measuring our skulls,
preparing for the long journey
            inland

Soft Metallic Voices

When the pleasure domes
      were no longer of interest

and the crowds had nothing more to say

the soft metallic voices
began their nightly visitations

creeping first in the depth of night
      then becoming daytime companions
      clicking and scratching
      deep behind the eyes

      electrical high voltage sparks
      raced across the cranium,
      jolting needles flashed inside the eyelids

These were the wake-up voices
      like interstellar pulses
      that snapped one to attention

Who could ignore voices
      even if they had nothing to say
      like the crowds in the supermarkets
      pushing the squeaky carts
      from aisle to aisle

All the while, waiting for a signal
      that revives the aspiring mind
      in its cortical folding
      and circuitry of wonder

Samsara

There will be those who understand
with little dust in their eyes.

Many more will remain
attached to clinging and aversion,
the source of disappointments,
running round and round
like dogs tethered to their pole.

Before earnest renunciation
there must come deep understanding of
impermanence in the world.

The shedding of skins
after long accumulation,
must touch the heart of compassion
as if after deep loss.

Glimpses of wisdom
will emerge like glints of light
as if rising from within
to be again rediscovered.

So much forgetting and falling down;
so much starting anew
and learning to let go again.

The Last Lost Time

I:
Forgetting for the moment
        all that we know

which is what we must do
        (and will do) at some point

let us agree that when the deer
        dances with the moon

this will be our signal
        to let go
        smother all the winds
        and remove any curiosity
        about where our intentions go
        when we abandon them

        there will be no hunter
        in this movement
        to slay the deer

back further to the largest pause possible

do you remember when we fell to our knees
        not in the safest place
        time moved slowly for us
        and our words slid out
                into the open spaces
                around us

there were other times where long pauses
        followed us into the desert

we ran through the sprinklers spraying water
          into the wind and wet college grass

gaps in time followed us as we made desert sand candles
          with fine grains like we found decades later
          along the Alabama Gulf Coast

Before we forget it all, let us reminisce further
          snippets and pastiche
          in summary, a collage in memory verses

you start first: yes, the coastal ferns and foxglove;

I remember it well, the fragrance of yarrow on the hillsides
          in coastal mist in quiet morning by Nepenthe
tide pools and the smell of kelp along cold coastline
          yes, the cool grayness was part of my memory too
          and do you remember the sea urchins closing
          at the slightest touch?

There were starfish and the feel of their stiffness. Farther back,
          abalone shells that were in your family
          going back a hundred years, picked up
                    on a California beach

This was before we ever heard of Ives' Unanswered Question,
          which to this day is a haunting probe into the past

and we tried to divine our fortune with yarrow stalks
          and we grew yarrow in our garden;
          it is the scent of memory like rosemary
          we saw cascading over the stone walls
          in Cambria or Mesa
          or was it later in . . . you may remember

but we are letting all that go
            aren't we?

We will let it stream out for a little while longer
            lingering in the fragrant evening
            as the cypress and junipers here
            and the tall grasses release their oils

Your downward look reminds me
            that we must also let go of the memories
            we have shared about all the friends and family
            that are no longer with us.

I agree this is hard, but you remember how it seemed
            difficult to discard our possessions at first,
            but once we started, it became easier

            The attachments to people we have loved
            continue to hold fast, even as we agree to let go

            It's the faces, at specific times, that I remember
            some are the painful last moments

            farther back are the better times, the innocence
                        we were fortunate to have

As we forget all that we know, that includes
            the words and their meanings

You know who I'm talking about in the family
            who forgot it all while she had to witness it in herself,
            even knowing that she was losing her own way,
            getting lost and having to agree to losing her driver's license,
            then—did she forget that she had agreed to come and live with us?

            Am I forgetting what actually occurred?

II:
I used to have words for these feelings?
        What is happening?

You're right. We're letting it all go.
        Did we agree to do this?

If we didn't, why is this, you know.
        Did you already take your slippers off?

You remember Uncle Johnnie? He wasn't the pharmacist, was he?
        Did he learn the slide rule? I mean slide trombone.
        I don't even remember what a slide rule is. I'm so stupid.

Go ahead, turn off the radio. I can't hear it right, anyway.
        These hearing aids aren't working. They don't fit right.

I wish they would stop that pounding on the ceiling.
        I'll have to wear one of those helmet things,
        you know that they strap to your head.

I used to have a scarf that was warm around my neck
        That was my favorite time. We used to dance till late
        in the morning. Johnnie Pancakes and his big band

You wouldn't know. I wish you had taken more interest in music
        instead of whatever it is you do.

III.
Those are the hardest memories of a mother to let go,
        because they are haunting, like Macbeth
                or was it Hamlet?

Sometimes it's like I'm in a stupor. I feel stupiferous
        like a Klondike Bar. Do you member—I mean remember—those

ice creams at the movie theaters? Those gummy ones—what were
  they—that stuck to your teeth? Abba Dabbas?

The pipe organs came out of the ground. Some people fell
into those orchestra pits.

It's sad how the mothers live so much longer alone.
      The husbands never know the pain they
      didn't have to endure. No, I didn't say enjoy!

Don't talk to me about those deep things.
      What do I know now about meaning?
      I hardly know my own name anymore.

The other day I was talking—oh look, there's one of those
      birds I saw the other day. What was I saying?
      See, this is what happens. It makes me so mad.
      I'm getting so stupid. This happened to Aunt Mary.

IV:
Tertinnium. I think it's tertinnium. My ears. Awful sound.
What did you say? Why are you looking at me like that?
Do you remember your father? You would have liked him.
He always dressed nice, even when he worked on the car.

Plurple. Plurple. What slikes; what slikes her in the house?

Domo Domo, sweet control oh! Feast and feist for Niagara Falls.
Rover, Rover come over. Sweet porkie pie.

Blah, blah, blah! That's all you say.
Don't take anything away from me.
It's mine. It's all mine.

More dribble on my chin.
Come over here, you!

Yeah, I'm talking to you.
I never liked you.

Blah, blah, block sheeps
Domo, Domo.
Plurple. Plurple

Evening at the Symphony

Violins, in their own language,
conveyed an anguish
that left us weeping.

How it transported us
            we do not know,
            but somehow,
            we knew this:

In time, our capacity to care
grew out of the pain
we observed in others.

Empathy and compassion
            rooted deep in ancient
            small wandering bands,
            led us to this evening's
            emotional tumult.

The orchestral strings tapped
on some human cord
like a symphonic tuning fork
adjusted to deep human sympathy
and we very quietly wept
those warm salty tears
and held back a choked
and convulsive breath.

The music of loss vibrated
inside of us in a recognition
that followed us all the way home.

We have cared for loved ones,
knowing all along
what the outcome would be.

We bottled our pain and loss
beneath a silent and stoic shell
until this evening,
when the violins in darkness
opened the chambers
of our guarded hearts,

and we sat until the early morning hours
at that same kitchen table
where so many remembered conversations
had occurred, unburdening the truths
that allowed us to move forward,
knowing that we did all
that we could have done
with no regrets.

Regeneration

Like the deer, we wandered
deeper into the woods to heal

Sitting and settling in
has been our way,
whether inside in comfort
or on a canyon trail
remote and far away
from the home and family
we once knew

Maybe seeing that the world around us
continues to move along
allows us to adapt again to its slow and peaceful rhythms.
The cypress and cedar do not bend to our sorrows;
the doe and her only fawn have their own concerns;
this helps in our own healing, a solace without words;
seeing that life around us exists only in the present.

In time, the breathing comes easier,
we begin to see more of the outward manifestations
on our hikes through mountains and deserts,
instead of the inward focus, the heavy feeling
that blinds us from where we are.

Even in its own suffering,
the green and growing world around us
heals us in its example of quiet persistence.

Today we noticed the new green shoots
emerging from the ground
after the rain three days ago.

Already, we are moving forward once again.

Sunset at Medina Highpoint

Letting go, dandelion seed fluff
      floats in the updraft,
      gliding above the treeline
      where hawks too
      swirl in long effortless ellipses
      leaving no imprint
      on the ground below

And here in a landscape of floating clouds
      people bring their troubles like shadows,
      unaware of the tall purple thistle blooming
      beside the swimming pool at sunset

I sit in a comfortable chair outside,
      cool breeze and a book
      beside the oak and cedar hillside,
      forgetting the noise when I can;
      not holding on—too much;
      letting go, with feet still on the ground,
      not yet the dandelion seed;
      no longer bringing troubles
      to this beautiful passing sunset;
      my footprint is smaller with each step,
      treading more softly as the years go by

Travel with Open Eyes

There will be whirlpools
that pull you in deeper
than any passing distraction;

the strongest is the invisible
seductive incantation of ideas
cloaked in knowledge and friendship,

sometimes irresistible when the guard
is down and people speak
in voices of certainty and trust.

When they put all their marbles
in one bag, it is because
they are desperate.

Superstition comes dressed
first as certainty, then as common sense
and unquestioned knowledge.

And still we walk along
and listen, pulled in by the eyes
we learned to trust long ago.

Sometimes we learn just in time
to let our judgments steep for awhile
like leafy tea in the cool morning air.

We push on, reminding ourselves
not to cultivate bitterness
and not doubt too much our own incantations.

Are we following some watercourse
meant just for us, we ask ourselves,
in a momentum that pulls us along.

We do not change our own stripes
and yet we are being transformed,
not so much by our passing encounters,

but by something vague and hidden
that occasionally reminds us
that any view has endless limitations.

Take this new hat that lends character
to those who place it on their head,
even when the head, itself, is unchanged.

How many hats we try on
in our meetings with others
and come away the same for it.

So we continue on, sometimes climbing,
sometimes falling, sometimes sitting still,
or shaking our heads at the unfolding spectacle.

Long before these travels
we were on a journey,
but when we rested so long in one place

or another, it seemed we were standing still,
but all the while, in retrospect now,
we were whirling in a kind of preparation

for this very moment, wherever we are,
dropping some of the burdens,
taking on new ones,

still learning what this traveling
in our house on wheels
is meant to be for us.

In our travels, as in life,
we do not know if we
are near any kind of end

or approaching a major transition,
because the illusion is
that this can continue forever,

but whether we are in spring
or autumn we know that eventually
the leaves will fall, and for us

we travel with the sun and the stars and the breezes
when we're fortunate to have them;
when we're buoyant enough to accept them.

To Hear the Wind and Seas

When the world is filled with ruthless words
sent swiftly and sharp as arrows,
piercing hearts across the world in an instant
before their consequences are considered,

it is time for us to retreat into the silent places,
to go back to the woods and the deserts,
to hear the wind and the seas once again
that communicate what words cannot.

We listen to the chorus of birds
who say much the same things to each other
that they have been saying as long as sky
and wings have existed together.

They figured out the essentials
and stuck to them since their origins;
theirs is not a language of progress
or domination or overwhelming the air waves.

Give us the rain and wind, the flowing waters,
the coyotes calling at dusk in the distance,
the hawk's music overhead in the canyons.

The curious child on the shoreline
explores with cupped hands
the play of sand and sea water,
in the wordless tide of pleasure.

We move through our landscapes,
darting in and out of the city of words,
meeting those whose hearts are yearning;
they too are members of our human flock.

We press on toward our simpler life,
no longer able to live apart,
so our departures are always temporary,
even if they are longer, like the fledgling flights
of those nested birds in the trees we find
in the wooded places, our adopted second homeland.

This effortless action of travel is not abandonment
as we come and go like the coastal tide waters
or the seasons that we follow in our course;
For now, we are guided in the updraft of warm currents
that carry us ever forward in this comforting flow.

Content with No Words

Sometimes content
        with no words

warm sun and soft breeze
        silence the thoughts

palm fronds set against blue sky
        in stillness high above
        offering companionship

past and future
        out of view
        beyond the distant horizon

lying here with a half-smile
sloughing off body and mind
        not even waiting
                for change

Late Night Cup of Tea

This contentedness may be fleeting, momentary,
        like the lull before
        the necessary occupations
        of the coming day

        but I am content with that
        at end of day
        feeling the tired calm
                that comes from working
                and walking

In our little house on wheels
        late at night
        I do a slow Tai-chi routine
        all incorrect and imitative,
        but flowing gently
        in comfort, alone
        a kind of slow jig for a tired man
        in a solitary moment

a calm conjuring of the muse
        while stilling the mind

a cup of tea waits at the table,
steeped leaves of mint and holy basil

such pleasure in this simple moment
late at night before writing this very poem.

Standing at McKinney Falls

Today I saw deep grooves
in solid volcanic rock
formed from the constant flow
of smooth and gentle water,
so refreshing against
bare stepping feet
crossing the upper falls.

For how many millennia
did the smooth caressing
and gentle touch
of flowing water
remove one grain here
or a fleck there of hardened stone
to sculpt rock so smooth and round,
and display to the casual observer
a scale of time
in which water dissolves rock
as surely as it does a salt lick
or sugar tablet?

The calculated measure of time
to remove the hardened rock
into these smooth and rounded grooves
above the waterfall
shows that rock too is like liquid
joining in the downward flow
of two local creeks conjoined.

The butter sculpture
at the county fair
melts in the summer heat
fast enough for us to see,
but the calendar

for this dissolving rock
beneath the water's steady flow
teases our human comprehension
as we marvel at its slow
and constant motion.

There is in this flow
of water rock time
the riddle for our contemplation:

Somewhere between the tiny gnat's
short passing view of a flower's summer bloom
and the rock's dissolving into the downstream sand flow,
all our human endeavors, loves, and sorrows,
are contained in time's cupped and curving crucible,
bending all appearances of beginnings and endings
into the dependent origination of all things,
the constant ebbing and flowing,
or an encircling ouroboros
onto which, for this little wondrous moment,
we cast these observing eyes.

Time Is a Mystery

Time is a mystery
      standing still as a glassy pond,
      or bending like river water
      curving smoothly over rounded stones

      never and forever
      slow and racing

      always tied to an observer
      like a kite string
      tugging at a paper dot
      fluttering and distant
      in the deep blue sky

With time, everything arises, intermingled
      in an instant of awareness

Time dissolves in late night's dreaming,
      or flashes like lightning
      to display long-lost memories
      some distance from the springs of Lethe

Time is wild, untamed, escaping capture,
      until the viewer's lights
      are once again extinguished

About the Author

Temporary, transient
passing through for a time
discarding accumulated acquisitions
holding on to some knowledge
glimpses of wisdom shared by others
sitting in deserts, climbing mountains
resting by the seashore
traveling with lifelong companion love
writing poems as reminders
of impermanence, patience, and gratitude
nothing special
sloughing off body and mind